©2018
Book Life
King's Lynn
Norfolk PE30 4LS

ISBN: 978–1–78637–258–1

All rights reserved
Printed in Malaysia

Written by:
Harriet Brundle

Edited by:
Kirsty Holmes

Designed by:
Gareth Liddington

A catalogue record for this book
is available from the British Library.

Photocredits: Abbreviations: l–left, r–right, b–bottom, t–top, c–centre, m–middle. All images are courtesy of Shutterstock.com.

Covert – Josep Curto, Coverm – Hurst Photo, Coverb – vivooo, 1 – Evan Lorne, 2 – rawpixel.com, 3 – Evan Lorne, 4 – SpeedKingz, 5 – Saroj Khuendee, 6 – Dmitry Kalinovsky, 7 – Silent Corners, 8 – Today ago kids, 9 – vchal, 10 – Jumnong, 11 – vilax, 12 – mtkang, 13 – Naiyana B, 14 – Cagri Kilicci, 15 – hxdyl, 16 – DenCake, 17 – Chinnapong, 18 – RoStyle, 19 – GOLFX, 20 – ITTIGallery, 22 – Monkey Business Images, 23 – Aleksandra Suzi, 24 – Albert Karimov.

Images are courtesy of Shutterstock.com. With thanks to Getty Images, Thinkstock Photo and iStockphoto.

CONTENTS

Words that look like **this** can be found in the glossary on page 24.

WHAT IS RUBBISH?

RUBBISH IS A TYPE OF POLLUTION.

When we no longer need something, we throw it away. This is rubbish. Rubbish can be anything from uneaten food to a broken toy.

Some of our rubbish, such as food, breaks down and disappears over time. Other rubbish, such as plastic, does not break down. This type of rubbish is more harmful to our **environment**.

WHERE DOES RUBBISH GO?

Our rubbish is collected and taken away every few weeks. The rubbish is taken to rubbish dumps, which are also known as landfill sites.

At landfill sites, our rubbish is put into huge holes in the ground. Once the holes are full, they are covered over with soil. More sites are then made.

RUBBISH AND
THE ENVIRONMENT

Landfill sites are bad for the environment. The rubbish can leak **chemicals** into the soil and nearby water. These chemicals can kill plants and are harmful to animals.

The rubbish can also cause air pollution because of the smell. Landfill sites are usually very unpleasant to look at too!

WOULD YOU WANT TO LIVE NEAR A LANDFILL SITE?

WHAT IS RECYCLING?

Recycling is the process of making our rubbish into something new so it can be used again.

WE CAN RECYCLE METAL TINS AND MAKE THEM INTO BIKE PARTS!

Lots of different **materials** can be recycled including glass, paper and plastic. By recycling, we can make sure that useful materials don't go to waste.

HOW DO WE KNOW WHAT TO RECYCLE?

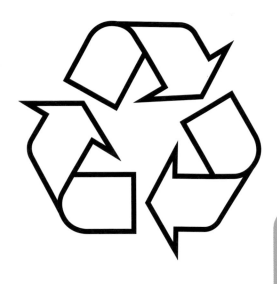

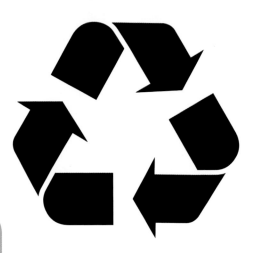

ANYTHING WITH THIS SIGN CAN BE RECYCLED!

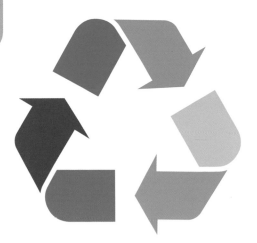

Lots of the things we buy have a symbol on them which tells us that they can be recycled. You can usually find the symbol somewhere on the **packaging**.

If something does not have the recycling symbol, ask a friend or adult if it can be recycled.

THINGS THAT CAN BE RECYCLED MUST BE PUT IN A SEPARATE BIN.

HOW ARE MATERIALS
RECYCLED?

Some materials, including glass and metal, are sent to factories where they are melted and made into something new.

Paper and cardboard are washed with chemicals to clean them and are turned into **pulp**. The sheets of pulp are then rolled out to make new paper and cardboard!

RUBBISH AND
RESPONSIBILITY

THE NUMBER OF PEOPLE LIVING SOMEWHERE IS ALSO KNOWN AS THE POPULATION.

As the world's population is growing, we make more and more rubbish.

We cannot carry on filling up landfill sites forever. It's important that we recycle as much as possible to look after our planet.

RUBBISH AND ANIMALS

Animals can think our rubbish is food. This can cause them harm. Rubbish can get stuck around an animal's head, leg or beak, which can stop it from being able to move or eat.

DON'T FORGET TO CHECK IF RUBBISH CAN BE RECYCLED BEFORE THROWING IT AWAY.

It is important we get rid of our rubbish in the proper ways so that animals are not affected. Always put your rubbish in the bin.

REDUCE, REUSE, RECYCLE!

Each day, we can lower the amount of rubbish we make by remembering this important saying: reduce, reuse, recycle!

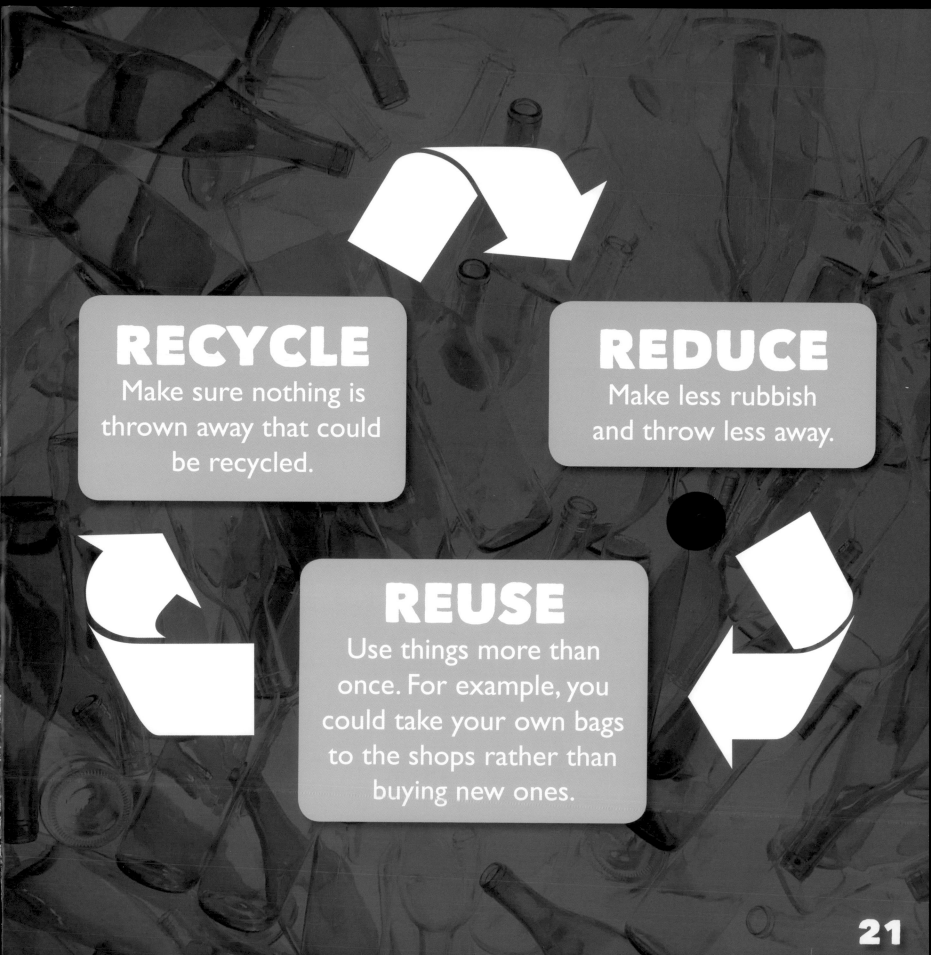

RECYCLE
Make sure nothing is thrown away that could be recycled.

REDUCE
Make less rubbish and throw less away.

REUSE
Use things more than once. For example, you could take your own bags to the shops rather than buying new ones.

HOW CAN WE HELP?

1. **Organise** a litter-picking event with your friends.

2. Look out for the recycling symbol whenever you put something in the bin.

REMEMBER TO ALWAYS WEAR GLOVES WHEN TOUCHING RUBBISH.

3. Try to make sure you have a separate recycling bin in your home.

4. Talk to your friends and family about remembering to reduce, reuse and recycle. The more people who know, the better!

23